CROSSFIRE

CROSSFIRE

Encounter with Friendly Fire: Handling Mishaps within the Christian World "For the flesh lusteth against the Spirit, and the Spirt against the flesh: and these are contrary the one to the other: so that ye cannot do the things that ye would." Galatians 5:17

Sheila A. Taylor

XULON PRESS

Xulon Press
2301 Lucien Way #415
Maitland, FL 32751
407.339.4217
www.xulonpress.com

Unless otherwise indicated, Scripture quotations taken from the
King James Version (KJV) – *public domain.*

Paperback ISBN-13: 978-1-66280-948-4
Ebook ISBN-13: 978-1-66280-949-1

ACKNOWLEDGMENTS

First, I would like to thank God for this project and giving me the courage to step out in faith.

I would like to acknowledge my good friends Elder E.N. and Evangelist Monica Parker for the support and helping me with the renaming of this project and lending their expertise.

Navarsha, my daughter in the Lord, and my niece Vanee' for reviewing and editing support.

Of course, to my loving husband David, who encouraged me and supported me in more ways than one. Thanks, honey, with much love.

Sheila

Contents

INTRODUCTION

SINCE THE BEGINNING of time there has been crossfires in families. In the first family of creation, there was a rivalry between Abel and Cain. The rivalry was so intense that it caused Cain to kill his own brother. Having said that, this booklet comes to help us to understand the crossfire that happens between the people of God. Traditionally, crossfire is just another way of saying friendly fire. Friendly fire is defined as a weapon coming from one's own side, and it can cause injuries within the body of Christ. With this definition in mind, I have found that it's the babes in Christ that are the most vulnerable to crossfire. Why do I feel they are the most vulnerable? Because of their innocence and ability to trust people that can cause them harm. Many times, this can cause them to not understand why they are feeling the heat of opposition from those who are supposed to be their spiritual family.

It is important to realize that many people never recover from friendly fire. Unfortunately, many times it's the so called "mature Christians" that tends to cause the cross-fire. We must be so careful not to wound the conscience of our fellow brethren. We must realize as Christians this is a continuous journey, that is never complete as long as we are above ground. We must work patiently with each other to ensure that crossfire does not crush the souls and enthusiasm of our brothers and sisters. *"If it be possible, as much as lies in you, live peaceably with all men"* [1] (*Rom. 12:18*).

The War

IT SHOULD BE noted that crossfire or friendly fire brings on war not in the faraway places you've read about but in the minds and hearts of believers. The Pharisees were known to inflict crossfire against our Lord Jesus. They got stirred up over the wrong things and caused their good work to be overshadowed by the kind of legalistic wrangling they were known for. In other words, they made a big deal over nothing. *"Ye blind guides, which strain at a gnat and swallow a camel"* *(Matt. 23:24)*. Jesus stressed that they needed to seek the things that were actually important as true Christians *(Matt. 23:23-24)*.

In our lives, we often come with our defenses up about the differences we share as Christians and do not know how to disagree in an agreeable way. God's truth is always the answer when we have conflicts within the body of Christ. *"If ye continue in my word,* **then are ye** *my disciples indeed; and ye shall know the truth, and the truth shall make you free"* (*Jn 8:31-32*). In addition, we need to stay focus on the renewing of our minds with the Word of God so we can be able to combat the wiles of the Devil and to prepare us to be aware of crossfire. *"And be not conformed to this world, be ye transformed by the renewing of your minds, that ye may prove what is the good, that acceptable and perfect will of God"* (*Rom. 12:2*).

MUTUAL RESPECT

WITHOUT A DOUBT, when dealing with cross-fire, respect is something everyone wants. Even a small child demands and deserves respect. It is unquestionably a common courtesy that is rendered with no expectation of receiving it in return, and while everyone wants respect, how do you get it? Like everything else in this world, you earn it! Remember the golden rule: *"Therefore all things whatsoever ye would that men should do to you, do ye even so to them"* (<u>*Matt.* *7:12*</u>). That does not mean that you will get the respect you want, but I believe that if you continue to do your part of showing respect, it will come back to you in return.

"Let us not be weary in well doing, for in due season we shall reap if we faint not" (<u>*Gal.* *6:5*</u>). I like to call this the rule of sowing and reaping: we are a product of what we produce.

That is why it is important to keep your mind renewed at all times. To avoid crossfire, we need to consider words like "thank you" and "please" to help us enhance the spirit of respect we give to those we encounter. Just because we are Christians, some people often think that they will be automatically respected but think again. Because the adversary is the author of confusion, he will not allow things to go smoothly. His motive is to *"kill, steal, and destroy,"* (**St John 10:10**). As Christians, we must strive to keep the unity of the faith intact. The door for crossfire opens every time we feel we have been disrespected. Remember unconditional love (Agape) is the key that will always unlock the door to mutual respect.

Watch-Your-Words

I REMEMBER WHEN they used to say, "Sticks and stones may break my bones, but words will never hurt me." This was a popular saying in the days of my youth. Unfortunately, it was never true. As Christians, we need to have control over our words and to watch what comes out of our mouth, however, it is easier said than done. *"Set a watch, O Lord, before; keep the door of my lips"* (__Ps. 141:3__). Controlling what you say will help you in the long run. The tongue can ignite arguments, fights, grumblings, and mumblings within the church (__James 3__), so controlling what you say is part of building your faith.

No man can tame the tongue; that's why we need to seek the Lord to help us with this problem. It is a small member of the body but can cause the most damage. Once you put words in the atmosphere, you cannot retrieve them back.

A lot of heartaches can result from being caught in the middle of words that can hurt. *"In the multitude of words there wanteth not sin but he that refraineth his lips is wise" (Prov. 10:19).* The words of our Lord Jesus himself taught about what defiles a man: *"Not that which goeth into the mouth defileth a man; but that which cometh out of the mouth, this defileth a man" (Matt. 15:11).* We must be careful of how we display our Christian graces through what we say because, **OOH-WEE!** Some of us can cast off a nasty, stinking attitude and we show it by the ugly words that we say. I was always taught, to think before you speak. Understanding that words we say have power and influence because life and death are in the power of the tongue.

INTIMIDATION

ANOTHER FORM OF crossfire is intimidation. According to the online version of the Merriam-Webster dictionary, the definition of intimidation is: **to frighten, make afraid** or *to make timid or fearful.*[2] We can experience spiritual peer pressure as Christians, and this crossfire can be extremely dangerous when you have been assigned by God for a special assignment. This type of coercion in the spirit can produce an unhealthy fear that can control us. Paul advised Timothy (Paul's son in the gospel) that being a new pastor, he would experience intimidation in his position due to his age. Paul expressed these words of encouragement to Timothy, *"For God has not given us a spirit of fear; but of power, and of love, and of a sound mind"* (*2 Tim. 1:7*). This still applies to our lives today. For example, when my husband became a pastor, I, of course, came along with him as a package deal. I experienced ridicule from other pastors' wives, leadership, friends, family, and even some members of the congregation. Women who were older than me would comment that I did not "look" like a pastor's wife or that they felt I was not capable of handling the job. This could have affected my faith and discouraged me not to accept the challenge of working alongside my husband to carry out the work that God wanted us to do together. The ridicule was horrible, but the Lord comforted me with the same scripture that Paul used to encourage Timothy (*2 Tim. 1:7*). Oh, what relief I felt! I placed that scripture in my heart, and the rest is history, and now, I am telling His-Story (preaching the gospel of Jesus Christ).

It's no fun being frightened because you fear people. Scripture teaches that we are not to fear those who can kill the body only but who can kill the body and soul and cast both into hell (*Matt. 10:28*). Fear paralyzes your ability to do what God wants you do. That is how the adversary, our bully, infiltrates and persuades us to do the opposite of what has been required by our Lord to do his will. Last but not least, it should be noted that people can try to make you feel inferior to them and act like they are superior to you. For example, you may play music, sing, or teach well, and if you serve in their church or under their leadership, they might exclude you purposely and not allow you to use the talent or gift the Lord has graciously given unto you to help enhance their ministry. If you accept the superiority complex they are trying to lay on you, then you will experience an inferiority complex. Again, we are not defined by people—you have a choice in the matter, and they do not set your destiny. You are in God's perfect plan, and as a true Christian, you are obligated to total obedience to the Lord's plan for your life.

Provide, Teach, Train, and Let Go

We must understand to keep ourselves out of the line of crossfire, we need to learn from nature. For example, mother birds provide food for their babies, teach and train them to survive, and then set them free to go out on their own. Likewise, the Bible teaches us (**2 Tim. 3:14-17**) to rely upon the Holy Scripture as our guide to help us grow and become equipped to do the work of God as well as, to avoid being harmed by crossfire. That is why it's important to be in a stable church home where teaching and preaching of sound doctrine of the Holy Scriptures are available for the growing and maturing Christian.

It is imperative that you continue in fellowship with the local church to help with your growth in the Lord. Faithfully studying the Scriptures is the perfect recipe for spiritual maturity and to help you combat crossfire.

Being a Christian is like being a college student. You **must attend school** to learn your major or vocation. You have to **invest** in books to study to learn how to do your profession. So, with that being said, as Christians, you **must attend church** to learn how to be a good Christian, and you must **invest** in a good study Bible and other resources in addition to the Bible to help you comprehend the Scriptures.

OPPOSITION OF CROSSFIRE

"IT WAS GOOD *that I was afflicted that I might know your statutes"* (<u>*Ps. 119:71*</u>). When we experience the crossfire of opposition, it is God's way of telling us that we need to move closer to Him. Opposition helps us to stay sharp and grounded in God's Word. It keeps us in prayer and prepares us to move forward in our lives, helping us to stay alert and on the lookout for the enemy of our souls. First Peter 5:9, says that we are a commodity for the enemy. He has his eyes on you, so do not become an easy target. If you suffer, you can reign with Christ.

Second Timothy 2:12, speaks about Christians suffering. We all want to see Jesus, but not all of us want to work for the kingdom to get there. Salvation might be free, but as someone said, it is not cheap. Jesus paid the price, and it costed Him his life.

It will also cost you your time, talent, and a few other things. It may even cost you your life. Remember! Only what you do for Christ will last. Just like a solider going to war, we must gear up. We must meditate on the word of God, practice Christian behavior, and make time to talk with Christ daily. Prayer is an essential discipline just like you routinely brush your teeth. We must fight our battles on our knees with all kinds of prayers, supplications, and intercessions. (*Phil. 4:6*).

RESPONSIBILITY OF
THE BELIEVER

ANOTHER FORM OF crossfire is when we are not united. Our Responsibility as believers is to maintain unity and peace among each other at all times (*Eph. 4:3*). We must understand where our place is in the Lord. When we cross lanes (doing the work that was assigned to someone else), we cause confusion, and mishaps within the body of Christ. Not knowing your place in the body of Christ can disrupt churches, relationships, and other areas of the Christian world. (*Eph. 4:1*). We as Christians are responsible for the work of the Lord. It is our responsibility to make sure that we are doing our part as committed Christians. It is not about you. It is all about Christ and His finished work. Knowing your place in the body of Christ make all the difference in the world.

Conclusion

In conclusion, we will always encounter crossfires. As believers, we must stay alert and sober to look for those pitfalls of trials that will come our way to get us off our target goal of serving Christ. Knowing this, we must always have a repentant heart and be in right relationship with Him while here on earth. Crossfire does not have to define you, but you can use it as a stepping stone only if used as a lesson learned. His finished work must be abiding in us as we continue to wait for the coming of the Lord.

~~~~

THE AUTHOR

EVANGELIST SHEILA TAYLOR is a native of Washington, D.C. She is a graduate from the District of Columbia public school system and has earned an A.S. in General Studies through the University of Maryland and Pima Community College of Arizona. She is also an alumnus of Andersonville Theological Seminary, where she earned a B.S. degree in Christian Education and an associate in Biblical Studies. In 1976, she dedicated her life after being witnessed to by David a neighborhood friend that had just dedicated his life to the Lord who later became her husband and now have been married over 43 years. She was called into ministry in 1985 and licensed as an Evangelist with Church of God in Christ (COGIC) while stationed in Stuttgart, Germany in 1988. The Lord has afforded her many opportunities to minister around the world. She now serves full time in ministry along with her husband Dr. David A. Taylor, who is

the senior pastor of Shiloh Ministries COGIC located in
Warner Robins, Georgia.

Why Now? When the COVID-19 pandemic began to spread in the United States in early 2020, I decided to keep myself busy and tackle something that I had been too busy to do. Writing this message was a dream I nurtured for many years (Since 2000). The crisis created an opportunity for me to minister in this way. The Lord allowed me to use this time to commit my thoughts to paper. I'm aiming to help Christians local and abroad, to understand the path to grow as a Christian, how to stay strong in this godly lifestyle and how to support the body of Christ without being trapped in crossfire. Believe it or not, you cannot be a wimp and be a Christian. It takes character and guts to stand against things that you do not see. It is definitely a different world (spiritual world) than the one we live in. Thank you Lord for allowing me to create this project in your name.

CONTACT US

Shiloh Ministries ~ Church of God in Christ (COGIC)
300 Ferguson Street
Warner Robins, GA 31093

Phone: 478-922-7629
Email: electladysheila@yahoo.com
Web: smcogic.com
(cover graphic)

ENDNOTES

1 All Scriptures provided King James Version, edition

2 Online Merriam-Webster Dictionary

9 781662 809484